THIS IS MY

"WILL"

How To Write Obiographical Sketches

[Your Own Obituaries]

The Resource Guide

Angelee Coleman Grider,

author

D1279158

Lizzie B. Dav__,

Funeral Director

THIS IS MY

"WILL"

How To Write Obiographical Sketches

[Your Own Obituaries]

The Resource Guide

Angelee Coleman Grider,
author

Lizzie B. Davis, Funeral Director

This Is My "Will"

How To Write Obiographical Sketches

(Your Own Obituaries)

©2007 M.O.R.E. Publishers
St. Louis, MO

M.O.R.E. Publishers Corp.

St. Louis, Missouri

©1990, 1996, 2007

(314) 383-7410

ISBN 978-0-9801647-7-0
Library of Congress Control Number: 2007909438
Printed in the United States

REFERENCE TABLE

PREFACE

THIS IS MY "WILL"! HOW TO WRITE OBIOGRAPHICAL SKETCHES (YOUR OWN OBITUARIES) is a handbook to help families and churches write creative obituaries for burial programs. The guidebook should be utilized before a death in the family.

The handbook is a new twist in preparing you to write more creative obituaries for burial ceremonies. The book includes a sample of a creative biographical sketch. Also included, for your convenience, are two forms that may be completed before beginning to formulate a final written copy of the obiographical sketch to be published with the program.

For your understanding, "Obiographical" means an obituary combined with a biographical sketch of a loved one. Let me help you to not be hysterical. Let's understand the word "obituary". An obituary is what you read in the newspaper announcing the end of life of a person. What your family wants to do is to write a true-to-life biographical sketch of your loved one. Write one that expresses the true person's ideas, as if he or she would tell them.

The handbook is intended to give you operational tools to use before an emergency. It is definitely needed during a time of decision-making. Begin by completing one of the enclosed forms, and then remember how the person spoke. Next, compose it as if the person is telling you his or her life story.

Read the examples for ideas. If the ideas don't come, don't worry. Ask the director to assist. All that is needed is the information in the booklet. If there are more details that you want to add, share.

DEDICATION

From Angelee

To my family who started our family tree.

As a result of those records, the several members of the family have developed three other publications: *BLACK TREASURE IN MISSISSIPPI AND THE BEST OF REVIVAL TIMES* (Florence W. Coleman); a historical developmental recordings of the family (Howard Wilkins); and *THIS IS MY "WILL"! HOW TO WRITE OBIOGRAPHICAL SKETCHES - YOUR OWN OBITUARIES* (by Angelee Coleman Grider and Lizzie B. Davis)

From Lizzie

To my family and especially my Aunt from whom I learned not to be afraid.

The Family Tree

(One of many deviations)

Family's Name_____

Your Name_____

Youngest child's name_____

Uncles, Aunts and Cousins

Nieces and Nephews

Great Grandchildren

Grandchildren

Children

Sisters and Brothers   Half sisters and brothers

Mother's Name

Father's Name

Introduction

No topic has ever been intriguing as the writing of personal obituaries. Saints, sinners, and others alike shun away from you at the mention of composing an authentic obituary before deceasing.

Please just think for a moment. Will parents, siblings, cousins and other relatives somehow get your intentions incorrectly once you are left on the mortician's tray with just a toe tag and cold body parts exposed for viewing by the undertaker? So to offset that "untimely death" confusion, write your own obituary in advance of all inevitable occurrences such as when one may be victim of comatose, paralyzation, or sudden human death.

At least if you prepare the "home-going" program ahead of time, no one will sing the inappropriate song that you told them not to sing as you said, "over my dead body." Nor can the will that you scribbled on a napkin be thrown into the trash can before you were willing to share the jewelry, famous liturgy never spoken but fantastically written, and how about this lovely sofa of which you just bought but planned to will it to Cousin Zulus. Though untimely, the truck came too swiftly. "Bam" was all that you can remember hearing before your pelvis was slithered into several pieces, right before you bled to death. You don't remember any of that do you? I hope not, because you are supposed to be dead. Now is this too gruesome for you? Please help me stop by trying to make a start in finishing your "will" and next your own obituary the way that you want it to be. Or if you want more than one, that's fine.

One woman told me she had surely written 12 of them. We should pray that she pinpoints which is the final decision. For the sake of humor, I can tell you, that it sure is okay to use all versions. We can console the family sometimes next year, after all of the programs.

Anyway, I told you that I encourage all who read this, to know there is a true time frame for anointing, for approaching the funeral director for pre-planned agreements and then wow, for giving burial directions about that mountain cliff where you desire your ashes disposed, or directions to the cemetery down in Kalamazoo (Mississippi). Either way it goes, your position will be stable on more decision-making things if you write your own "home-going" program.

I don't want to talk about the burial place, but the more you learn, the better decisions you are equipped to make. Did you know that the cemetery plot is not included in the funeral costs? That's right, after you spend all of that money, sometimes $30,000 for just funeral programs, newspaper announcements and deceased flowers, you still will have no where to go until you pay for some "dirt" to be thrown over your remains. So, let's talk "dirt."

Be hospitable to one another without grumbling^ When you no longer can stop the family feuds in person, what do you think they are going to do? Yes, they will start grumbling about what you should have left them. This is "dirty" talk. You most certainly do not need the grumbling before you are down in a deep sleep – resting. So let's make it easy on you. Write the will. Leave a note somewhere and say, "This is my will!" Add a little humor and say, "all rights reserved".

What can go in your will? First, remember that you should have sought legal advice before you decided to check out of the Body Hotel. The legal system answers this question better than I can. I will only share with you what I heard and researched. Keep in mind, while you are alive, that this handbook is in no way meant to be a legal source of directions. Always seek counseling from professionals in different areas. My expertise is in the writing and communication. To help you out, I did consult with Lizzie. So read on and learn more.

^1 Peter 4:9 – The Gideons International

Angelee Coleman Grider

An Obiographical Sketch Example

"My Day"

Born on the 9th day of May and a "hell raiser" then, I was determined to be a preacher for God. My mother, Mary, of the Ownes family, left records that informed me that Catholic General was my birthing place, in a small one-hoe town of Macon, Georgia. Daddy, Mott C. Moody, married Mom and decided to cease having children. I was an only child.

Lord, but would you believe that after I married Lois Mayweather, we brought forth Martha who is still living in California; John, a resident of Michigan; and Florence, a native of Oklahoma. As a result of these, we have 29 grandchildren. Oh, I also must mention that I'm leaving 14 cousins, 9 uncles, and 12 aunts to bury me.

Enough about my family, you came to read about me. I confessed to being a preacher at the age of 14, at Mt. M.B. Sanctuary, where I am still a member until after tomorrow. I was a deacon, an assistant to the Sunday school minister, a member of the choir, and a member of the usher board.

All in all, I guess you could say that I've led a "pretty good" life. After all, I enjoyed it, for "Life was too short to be wasted."

What Happens When Lizzie Takes Over?

While sitting in a car outside of a St. Louis library in Baden, April 19, 2007, Lizzie dictated while I wrote. She kept saying, "Don't forget to tell them..." You see, Lizzie is an "undertaker". Interesting how that term says it all. By definition, Lizzie and her associates are the ones who will "take you under" the ground. However, she said that there were some things that you needed to prepare in advance.

First, she emphasized that all families needed a "FAMILY TREE". This should be completed effectively with no incorrect spelling of names. Be careful not to put the wrong person in the wrong family. When your family brings the copy to the counseling office, the publisher will only print whatever is listed. There won't be time for researching.

Had you ever wondered why most burial programs or notification announcements in the paper usually states, "a host of nieces and nephews"? One reason, by all means is because someone wished that they had a list of all the cousins and stepchildren. Rather than offend anyone by omitting their names, they use the word "host". This means "I can't remember all of your names, and the half that I don't even know about, I'm sorry but I don't have time to try to find you." The program must go on.

In fact, Lizzie said, "Don't forget..." to tell you that you don't need to embalm a person, you just have to remember that remortilization is about to occur, and the body will surely start decomposing all by itself. Therefore you only have a short time to get the body back to the rightful owner, the earth. See, talking dirt is not as bad as it sounds.

ADDING UP THE COST

I was just informed that the price of country-yard cemetery plots has increased by $400.

Ask for the GPL. Lizzie said to tell you to ask for a General Price List from the Director of Counseling. According to Lizzie, this list includes everything that is sold from the Directors and anything that is not on that list should not be sold. If there is a non-listed item offered to you or someone in the family, it is considered an unethical, not to mention an illegal practice.

Don't forget the following:

1. Pre-need policies can be used as insurance policies anywhere. It's just insurance.

2. The pre-need insurance policies are for the policy owner, not the beneficiary. The beneficiary was named as "caretaker" to do the right thing when it is time to bury the owner of the policy. Other life insurance policies may be secured in order to leave financial security to the family. The obligation to bury the person comes out of the money first.

3. Regardless of how much you do or don't like someone, the legal rights go first to the husband or wife if the person is lawfully married. The Director of Counseling will honor decisions made by them.

4. Embalming is crucial if you plan to hold off having the services a day or two trying to wait until someone arrives in town. Embalming is not mandated. However, if you are trying to avoid the cost of embalming, you must remember that the body must be put into the ground immediately. The next day would be quite appropriate, but you probably will not be able to have an opened-casket funeral. Bodies decay very fast.

5. Make a list of wishes while you can think straight.

6. If the person is a serviceman or woman, or a veteran, it is highly recommended that you place these papers in a safe, convenient place. When necessary you will find them. Be able to ask for proper plot location, and ask for a flag for the coffin and to keep as a memorial after the eulogia service.

7. To omit family feuding and name-calling, pick out your own cemetery plot. This is a separate contract with cemetery owners. The Director will only give a list of recommendations. This cost will not be found on the GPL form. If it is, ask who owns the cemetery.

8. Do you want the religious creation, standard service? Do you want to be cremated? Make a decision now so you will truly understand what is involved in the cremation process. Services generally begin at $695.

9. Don't count on the State burying you. Or do you not mind being thrown on top of someone else's body? Do you mind your remains resting in a cardboard box? If all of this sounds disgusting, you need a pre-need plan in place for your service, burial, and after-tax expenses.

10. Do ask for counseling. At this moment you need someone to listen to you. You need to fully understand what you are doing before the service. The family needs counseling to help heal after grieving. Talk to someone in a professional capacity. Many Directors of Counseling are now equipped to offer the grief counseling service. If not, someone will be recommended. Enjoy life and get your affairs in order. What's more important – loving someone and putting a responsibility on them that truly they don't deserve, or is it more important to love them and have a plan? Just label your request and say "This Is My Will!"

Personal Preference

Don't forget to contact the hairdresser for the ladies. Bid for competitive service, but if the pre-need specifies, get the family beautician. If a hat is wanted, bring the prettiest one unless a certain one has already been chosen. Men may also like a certain look from their Saturday morning barber. If so give him a call. If he says 'I'm sorry to hear the news", you say "God would want you to be a servant until the end." Then give him/her the address where to conduct the haircut and shave service. The counseling director will take over from there to complete the final facial, body, and final visitation and burial service favorite clothing attire preparations.

UNIVERSAL FIGHTS OVER OTHERS' INSURANCE

1) Whose name is listed on the policy?

2) Who is the beneficiary?

3) Who was really the caretaker?

4) For whom is the money really to be used?

First, it is your responsibility to either have enough funds on hand or good "rich" family members to provide for a funeral that is befitting your choice of "home going". Secondly, if you are apt not to have saved enough funds, your closet on-hand cash is going to be used from your burial policy.

Therefore, your name will be on the insurance policy as the "owner." Then you must decide who it is in the family or in your circle of friends that you will be able to trust, once you are not to say anything. Does this person care about you now? Is the person responsible with his or her own funds? However, if the designated person never seems to have any funds, but when emergencies arise he/she steps up in the leadership role and does what is right, then choose that person.

Before allocating responsibilities, you personally need to know what the different terms mean. "Burial Policy" is "insurance". "Life Insurance" is "insurance". "Term Life" is "insurance" that is extended for a certain period of time. The owner must decide how long to keep paying on it. "Whole Life" is "insurance". You basically don't stop paying on it. You pay for it your whole life.

"Credit Life" is "insurance". It is the money that can only be used to pay for bills that you may have. You will have bills left. Regardless of what "they" say, hospital bills don't mysteriously go away after the sick person dies. The ambulance bill doesn't disappear either.

"Accident Insurance" is only worth the ink that is used to write the policy. Unfortunately, if you do not die from an accident, you won't get any funds.

Find someone to write a policy for you. Find someone who throws no curve balls, but straightforward tells you what you don't want to talk about, but what you definitely need to know.

For the sake of your family, you should find a credible plan. Family members will of course ask did you have "insurance" so they won't need to spend their "hard-earned-money" to funeralize you nor to bury you. They will certainly not want to pay to cremate you either. Find a reliable beneficiary.

A beneficiary, by law, does not need to be just one person. If you find out that you are going to need only $15,000 to bury you decently, and you will leave $39,000 behind, "Scott Free", you may want to name and divide the sum into three parts: the spouse, children, and a church organization. This is just an example.

Be careful! Be careful! Be careful! Be careful not to omit the person's name of the one who has torn their life apart and was willing to take care of you during your lifetime. True love is better than any sacrifice at a funeral. Take the time to read your policy and revise it if necessary. Surely you would not want to realize on the day that you are dying that you left a dead body's name on the policy. It is a shame too if your nurse went beyond his/her call of duty to care for you, even on off days, and you only thought to say thank you, but you left all of your money to the sister who visited once during the several times when you were in a convalescent home.

Another thing to remember is that if you forget to pay on the policy, after the grace period, the company will have no mercy on you. You will have wasted all of that time and funds for no reason. Be sure that if you apply for insurance policies, you plan to keep them "alive" until you die. If you are a "high-risk" person, start saving large sums of money, stay healthy, or never let the policy lapse. Stay in contact with your agent or company. Representatives are good to contact when you no longer remember that the premiums are going to rise as you get older, approximately every five (5) years.

If the breadwinner dies before you, soon it will become apparent why your agent said the policy was "income protection", for now you no longer have a good income.

Remember that regardless of how much money is allotted to the beneficiary, the funds really are intended to use for the final care of the owner of the insurance policy. It's not yours about which to fight amongst the family.

CREMATION

The fire popped quickly from the side carport wall. It was coming from the socket. In my mind I should have thought to run to a neighbor's house for assistance or resource material. With the coat that I had on my back, I flapped at the flames. Then the coat caught on fire. "Move the car!" the small voice of the Holy Spirit whispered to me.

I ran inside for I thought that if I could not save the house, I would not be able to explain why I did not save my son's car. So I ran in the house, grabbed the keys, and moved the car from out of the path of the flaming fire. I ran back to the side of the house. The flames miraculously did not engulf me. As I threw the coat again at the fire, which was still contained on the outer wall, fire popped at me. I jumped back. Hot plastic-like substance hit my hand. It burned! Burned! Burned! If I feel like this now, I thought, how can someone want to be cremated?"

Cremation is the process of the burning of the body's skin and flesh. Lizzie said that the bones would need to be crushed. They don't burn very well. So when you receive someone's remains, you are getting bone fragments to disburse among the ground. That's what Lizzie said.

SAMPLES

Obituary and Forms

In Loving Memory

of the late

Mr. Aaron Wilkins I

Æ

Thursday,

February 14, 1980

1:30 p.m.

Mt. Pisgah C.M.E. Church

Cayce, Miss.

Rev. A.D. Warren, Sr. Pastor

Rev. W.C. Armstrong, Presiding Elder, Officiating

An Obituary

"My heart is ready, O God, My heart is ready!" Psalm 109

For I, Aaron Wilkins 1 was like any mortal man.

I WAS BORN.   Life was given to me on March 19, 1893, in Marshall County, Mississippi.   I, Aaron, or "Buddy" as some called me, was the son of Eli and Virginia Wilkins.   I was placed in a family of four brothers, John Wilkins, Henry Washington, David and Ivory Smith.

I LIVED.   And as I lived, I gave my life to God by becoming a Christian at the age of 14 and served as a shepherd at Mt. Pisgah C.M.E. Church for 73 years.   I labored as president of the steward board, president of the trustee board, church treasurer, and class leader.

Also to my blessed life I was united with Ora Moody Wilkins my devoted wife of 65 years.   To fulfill that union God loaned us our children Mrs. Mary M. Kizer, Mrs. Della Wadsworth Phillips, Ms. Ada Wilkins Wilkins (deceased), Mrs. Florence W. Coleman, Rev. Aaron Wilkins II, Mr. James Wilkins, Rev. Cleveland Wilkins, Mr. Herman Wilkins.

Sustaining a long life of 87 years, I witnessed three generations with 50 grandchildren and 32 great grandchildren.

I also shared the company of 5 sisters-in-law, 3 brothers-in-law, 1 aunt, 2 uncles, 4 daughters-in-law, 2-sons-in-law, 20 nephews, 20 nieces, and a host of other relatives and friends.

I DIED.   God spoke and I was silent.   On February 10, 1980, my soul returned to Him.   Man said I ceased to exist at 8:45 a.m., but only I and God know the exact time I was rendered to eternal life.

No longer now shall you hear my frail voice sing "Turn That Key Around" on this unclean world that you must still roam, for God has turned His own eternal golden key and called another child on home.

Order of Service

Rev. A.V. Warren

Processional

Song... Choir

Prayer...…...Rev. A.V. Warren

Scriptures

Song ....….. Bro. Clarence Watson

Remarks: (limit 2 minutes)

Bro. Louis Hines ....…....................……........... Steward Board

Bro. Kelsey Kizer ....….. Neighbor

Community

Solo ....…............. When I Am Gone ... Bro. Ruby Butler

Acknowledgements and Obituary ....…....…....Bro. Johnny Hines

Hymn ....Another Soldier Gone ....…....... Bro. Edward Dean Garrison

Remarks ....…....…........ Rev. Paul Buchanan

Eulogy ....….. Rev. W.C. Armstrong

Viewing of the Remains

Recessional

Going Home

INTERMENT

Mt. Pisgah Cemetery

ACTIVE PALLBEARERS

Aaron Wilkins III	Milton D. Wilkins
C.L. Wilkins	Alton Kizer II
L.B. Wilkins	Rev. George Coleman Jr.
Bradford Wilkins	

Grandsons of the late Mr. Aaron Wilkins I

HONORARY PALLBEARERS

Steward Board Members of Mt. Pisgah Church

FLOWER BEARERS

Granddaughters of the late Mr. Aaron Wilkins I

Patty L. Wilkins	Ora M. Wilkins
Catherine D. Wilkins	Diane Wilkins
Charlean Wilkins	Dorothy W. Garrison
Velvet Virginia Lee Wilkins	Mary E. Kizer
Darleen Wilkins	Brenda L. Wilkins

ACKNOWLEDGEMENTS

Words cannot convey our deep gratitude and appreciation for all of the expressions of kindness and sympathy shown us during our hour of need. Your visits, telegrams, flowers, and every act of kindness, and prayers will serve to brighten the lonely days ahead. May God bless each of you?

J.F. Brittenum & Son Service
Holly Springs, Mississippi

Holly Springs Printing Company

OBIOGRAPHICAL SKETCH FORM

(List)

Person's name:_____

Present age:_____

Date of birth: Month_____ Day__ Year___

Place of birth: City _____

                    State_____

Friends: How many? _____

Special Friend: _____

Wife's name: _____

Husband's name: _____

Is the wife/husband living?   ___yes   ___no

Children: Where they live:

1. _____   City_____ State_____

2. _____   City_____ State_____

3. _____   City_____ State_____

4. _____   City_____ State_____

5. _____   City_____ State_____

6. _____   City_____ State_____

7. _____   City_____ State_____

8. _____   City_____ State_____

9. _____   City_____ State_____

10. _____   City_____ State_____

Occupation: _____

Business Name: _____

Address: _____

Phone: _____

Religious: ___yes   ___no

Name of church: _____

Pastor's name: _____

Important Phone Number _____

Position in the church:

       ___bench member   ___deacon

       ___elder   ___steward

       ___stewardess   ___usher

       ___mother   ___choir member

       ___pianist   ___director of _____

       ___president of _____

       ___other (name) _____

Favorite song: _____

Favorite scripture: _____

Favorite words: _____

Favorite color: _____

Favorite activity: _____

Nickname: _____

Day of immortality: _____

Stated, Recorded Time: _____

Place of physical departure: _____

Reason/ cause: _____

_____

Number of Relatives:

(List on the Family Tree".)

    1. cousins: _____

    2. aunts: _____

3. uncles: _____

4. grandchildren: _____

5. great-grandchildren: _____

6. nieces: _____ and nephews: _____

Names of sisters:

_____

_____

_____

Names of brothers:

_____

_____

_____

Favorite testimony:

_____

_____

_____

_____

_____

_____

OBIOGRAPHICAL SKETCH FORM

(Written Paragraph Form)

_____ (name) was a devoted

_____ and _____.

On _____ at _____A.M./P.M. (date),

_____ (name) was changed to
immortality.

_____(name) was

loved by ___ children, ___ friends, ___ cousins, ___ cousins,

___ nieces, ___aunts, ___uncles and ___grand-children.

The children born to _____ (name)

were _____

_____ and

_____.

One thing he/she always said was _____

_____

_____.

This was a true expression of character displayed

through his/her love of _____ (scripture)

and _____(song).

_____'s (name) last

words of wisdom were _____

_____.

You could say that_____ (name)

was/was not a religious person. He/she held active

membership/position as _____,

_____, and as

_____.

He/she worked as a/an _____,

_____,

and _____.

The church that he/she worshiped in for _____

years was _____

of which Rev. _____

was the pastor.

Analysis of Your Situation

Current Income_____

Unearned Income_____

Monthly bills and expenses_____

Debt reduction_____

Savings_____

Investments_____

Other Assets_____

Current Debts_____

Mortgage Balance_____

Current market value of Home_____

Purchase Price of Home_____

Equity_____

Life Insurance_____

Health insurance_____

Disability insurance_____

Home insurance_____

Auto insurance_____

Retirement savings_____

College savings_____

Total Money Saved _____

Total Money Spent_____

Total Needed_____

Where are your receipts?

LIFE INSURANCE POLICY

_____

_____

MILITARY FORMS

_____

_____

BANK ACCOUNT CHECKS

_____

_____

OBITUARY

_____

WILL(S)

_____

WEDDING PAPERS

_____

An Analysis

1) Income per month _____

   Other sources of income _____

   Total Amount _____

2) 5% of Income _____ (savings)

3) 10 Income _____ (savings)

4) Three (3) months income _____ (savings)

5) Savings Account amount _____ (savings)

Insurance

REMEMBER:

1) Husband and wife's name must be on the beneficiary sheet.

2) What is your social security number?

   _____

3) What is your driver's license number?

   _____

4) Who normally writes the checks?

5) Who will write the checks if you are incapacitated?

6) Is your insurance paid from your direct deposit account?

7) Do you still have insurance policies for your children? Where are the policies located?

8) Did you pay your annual taxes?

9) If you become disabled, before death, you may ask for a percentage of the life insurance to help pay for medical bills.

10) Money needed at the time of someone's death is as follows:

    a. funeral expenses

    b. cemetery expenses

    c. lawyer expenses if there is a will

    d. emergency funds

    e. debts

    f. mortgage

    g. education funds if there are children

    h. car note (if there is no credit life insurance or if the car is not paid in full)

    i. business income if there is a company

    j. estate taxes

MASTER CHECKLIST

Check off and initial each item as it is accomplished.

Place an "X" in the box if it does not apply to the situation

ACTION	BY WHOM	DOCUMENTS	BY WHOM	DATE
Clergy Notified		Death Certificate Filed		
Organist Notified		Funeral Contract Signed		
Hairdresser Notified		Burial Permit Obtained		
Active Pallbearers Notified		Certified Copies Ordered		
Honorary Pallbearers Notified		Social Security		
Vault Ordered		Social Security		
Police Escort Arranged		V.A. Flag Obtained		
Newspaper Obituary Given		V.A. Burial Allowance Application Mailed		
Newspaper Funeral Notice		Statement Mailed/Presented		

Given				
Cemetery Personnel Notified		Claim Filed Against Estate		

Definitions

Will – Desired written statements of what property to have disbursed to others after you are no longer alive.

Things to remember about a will:

1. If you have a will you will go through probate court.

2. An attorney should design the will to make sure your property is divided equally.

Financial Needs Analysis – a form analyzed upon completion, used to determine the status of a person's finances. This includes a person's income, assets, expenses, liabilities, net worth, insurance policy value, and long-range goals.

Funeral Counselor - a slight elevation from a director; yet more personally focused on helping the family through a rough time. The counselor is available for consultations, sessions and for those who just need to talk, before and after the arrangements. Counselors are either certified directors and counselors, or specialists, therapists, or certified state counselors.

References:

HOW TO WRITE OBIOGRAPHICAL SKETCHES,

> Angelee Coleman-Grider, M.O.R.E. Publishers, P.O. Box 38285, St. Louis, MO, ©1990, 1996, (314) 383-0851, www.MOREPublishers.biz

THE GIDEONS INTERNATIONAL,
2900 Lebanon Road, Nashville, Tennessee 37214, ©1985.
www.gideons.org

1995 Undertakers customer service guide

Prices are subject to have changed as of this reference.

Casket price x 8% = Tax

Insurance = 6%

Casket price x 3 (markup) + 2885 + Tax + 6% = Total price – tax – casket price = package price

Example:

$10,348.28 (pkg.) + $266.96 (tax) = $13,952.74

Undertaker caskets can be returned if you change your mind before actually using the item, if you have the proper invoice.

Sample Prices:

Bronze with metal inner panel $13,500

Bronze without metal inner panel $12,500

Bronze Shell $ 5,700

Stainless Steel $5,600 -$6,600

Mahogany (wood) $ 4,906

Colors and texture range from velvet (beige, burgundy, blue, ivory) to brushed gold

INFORMATION NEEDED TO COMPLETE THE DEATH CERTIFICATE

1) Name of the deceased _____

2) Address_____

3) Date of birth_____

4) Place of birth (city)_____

5) Place of birth (state)_____

6) Spouse's full name (including the maiden name)_____

7) Father's name_____

8) Deceased's social security number _____

9) Veteran's discharge papers _____

10) Church affiliation_____

11) Member of what "Orders" lodges, societies, etc.

_____

12) Survivors' names and their relationship (including city of residence)

_____

13) Location of chosen funeral service_____

14) Date and time of desired funeral service_____

15) Location of cemetery_____

16) Name of minister_____

17) Which special choir?_____

18) What special music?_____

19) Active   and   honorary   casket   bearers:

_____

_____

20) Active   and   honorary   flower   bearers

_____

PAPERWORK NEEDED:

1. Recent photograph

2. Insurance

REIMBURSEMENTS

1) NO reimbursement for a beneficiary if the service fee exceeds the amount of the insurance policy.

2) NO reimbursement for a parent of a descendant under 21 years old.

TIME LIMITATIONS

30 days to claim remaining items (watch, purse, etc.)

180 days: claims will be denied (no merchandise will be given)

90 days to resubmit claims if claimant must correct information

VETERANS ADMINISTRATION BENEFITS

- $300 for burial and funeral expenses

- $150 for internment (burial)

- Free internment if in a national cemetery. Or other cemetery under the jurisdiction of the United States.

- $150 paid to a State or State agency or political subdivision, if a veteran died from non-service-connected causes (example whooping cough)

- Free internment of the deceased if the body will be buried in a state-owned cemetery, or if the person was eligible to be buried in a National cemetery

- Up to $1,000 when death occurs as a result of a service-connected disability (example - gun-shot wound that did not heal)

SOCIAL SECURITY ADMINISTRATION BENEFITS

$255 generally as a lump sum (only given to an eligible surviving spouse or legally entitled child)

FEES

1) services

2) Merchandise

3) Late penalty payment

4) % per annum on unpaid balance

5) Payments by estate collateral must be paid by a family member in advance and then collected after the reading of the will, etc.

TERMS OF PAYMENT

1) up-front payments before the funeral

2) cash advances

3) bank or credit union financing

4) Master Card

5) Visa

6) Discover

7) Verified insurance benefits

All balances must be clear before the services and burial.

GENERAL PRICE LIST (GPL)

Prices subject to have changed since publication date of this book.

Policy: Goods and services listed in a Director's GPL are those that can be provided to the customers. A customer may choose only the items desired. Prices included are only for basic services and overhead. If legal or other requirements mean that a customer must buy any items not specifically asked for, the Director must explain the reason in writing on the statement provided, describing the funeral goods and services that the customer selected.

BASIC SERVICES OF FUNERAL DIRECTOR, STAFF AND OVERHEAD

1) a conference

2) planning the funeral

3) consultation with the family and clergy

4) shelter for the remains

5) preparing and filing of necessary notices

6) obtaining necessary authorizations and permits

7) coordinating with the cemetery

8) crematory

9) negotiating with third parties

10) basic overhead

SERVICES (Sample Prices)

Embalming (not required by law)	**$435**

Preparation of the body

Reconstructive restoration when necessary	**$ 50**
Hair Dresser	**$ 50**
Special care of autopsied remains	**$ 55**
Washing and disinfecting (no embalming)	**$100**
Dressing and casketing (unembalmed)	**$ 50**

Transfer of remains to funeral home

Within 50 mile radius	**$200**
Beyond 50 miles = $4 per mile	
Use of Director's Facilities and Staff (viewing)	**$200**
Use of Director's Facilities and Staff (ceremony)	**$200**
Use of Staff and Equipment (church viewing)	**$200**
Use of Staff and equipment (church funeral)	**$200**

Use of equipment and staff (burial)	$200
Funeral car for casket	$175
Limousine	$175
Caskets	$269 - $13,000
Monograms	
Initials only	$ 15
Full name	$ 30
Full name, date of birth and date of death	$ 35
Outer burial container	$435 - $14,000
Forward remains to another Director	$650
Receive remains from another Director	$795
Direct Cremation	
1) With container provided by purchaser	$750
2) With Fiberboard	$895
3) With an unfinished wood box	$995

IMMEDIATE BURIAL

1) No ceremony, with casket provided	$1,380
2) Alternative container (if offered)	$1,695
3. cloth-covered wood casket	$1,830

CASH ONLY

1) Flowers (generally 3-piece family floral) $215

2) Clergy $ 50

3) Musician $ 50

4) Death Certificates $ 10

5) Standard Printed Programs   (300 copies) $110

DIRECTOR'S SERVICES (general)

1) Director and staff consultations

2) Transfer of remains to funeral home

3) Embalming

4) Other preparation of the body (such as cleaning)

5) Use of facilities for 1 day

6) Funeral car for transportation of body

7) Committal or other disposition service

8) Acknowledgement cards

9) Prayer cards

10) Visitors' register book

11) three to four limousines

12) One additional facility usage $11, 935.09 - $30,000

VIDEO TRIBUTE

Included are family photographs and other visual documentations. Usually has background music.

Samples:

1) 1-15 pictures $150

2) 15-30 pictures $295

THIS IS MY "WILL"

Name of Counselor or Director

_____

I, _____, (your name)

Being in my right frame of mind, request the following attire:

1) **Underwear**_____

2) **Shirt or blouse**_____

3) **Slip**_____

4) **Shoes** _____

5) **Suit**_____

6) **Dress** _____

7) **Socks** _____

8) **Glasses**_____

9) **Earrings**_____

10) **Makeup**_____

Name of Beautician or Barber

_____

Address or Phone Number_____

Name of Musician _____

Phone Number_____

Name of clergy for the eulogy_____

PRE-PLANNED SERVICE INFORMATION

Total cost of funeral service $_____

Total cost of burial $_____

Director's costs $_____

Amount already paid $_____

Insurance Policy Amount $_____

Insurance Policy Amount $_____

              Balance Due $_____

INSURANCE

Company Name_____

Policy Number_____

Amount available $_____

Beneficiary (after you pay my bills)

_____

Company Name_____

Policy Number_____

Amount available $_____

Beneficiary Name(s) (after you pay my bills)

_____

_____

ARRANGEMENTS

(To Be Completed By the Director or Counselor)

Date of Funeral _____

Place of Funeral _____

Date of Death _____

Time of Death _____

Time of Funeral _____

Date of the Awakening Service _____

Place of the Service _____

Time _____

Visitation Date and Hour(s) _____

Pick up time for funeral service _____

Burial area _____

City _____ State _____

Town _____

Name of Cemetery _____

Location _____

FEDERAL TRADE COMMISSION DISCLOSURE AND/OR DISCLAIMER FORM

The Federal Trade Commission's Funeral Industry practices Rule requires that certain disclosures be made to avoid misrepresentations.

Please read and sign the following.

Name _____

Date of death _____

1) A General Price List was given before discussing prices, services, merchandise, or arrangements
_____initials

2) A Casket Price List was given before the viewing or discussion of prices of caskets

_____initials

3) An Outer Burial Container Price List was given before viewing or discussing prices of outer burial containers
_____initials

4) I understand that law except in certain cases does not require "embalming"; therefore if it is done, it is by permission of the representative present

_____initials

5) I understand that we are entitled to disposing of the body by "direct cremation", "immediate burial", or "refrigeration" if available. There will be no further public viewing of the body or visitation services.
_____initials

6) It is clear that the law does not require the purchase of a casket for direct cremation.

_____initials

7) It is clear that the law does not require the purchase of an "outer burial container"
_____initials

8) The Director or Counselor or no Representative made any statement that embalming or the use of any merchandise available from the Director's facilities would delay the natural decomposition or disposal of the remains for a long period of time or for an indefinite period of time. _____initials

9) I understand that the Director or Counselor of the facilities named _____

disclaimed all warranties with regard to caskets, outer burial containers, and other merchandise sold by the Director or the staff of the facilities.

10) I am aware that there are no warranties, including expressed warranties, implied warranties of merchantability or fitness for particular purposes have been offered to the facility and staff. I understand there are only certain written warranties from the manufacturers of products used

_____initials

My name_____

Date_____

Attendant's Signature/Legal Guardian

_____

Date_____

My Signature_____

Today's Date_____

Waiver of Statutory Right to Make Funeral Arrangements
And Designate Final Disposition

AFFIDAVIT OF WAIVER

I, _____ (name)

The undersigned, which is the legal (circle one) guardian,
spouse, child or other (specify) _____

In relationship to _____

NAME OF PERSON NEEDING SERVICES

In consideration of funeral services and burial
arrangements to be performed by

_____

(BUSINESS NAME)

do hereby waive my/our legal right to designate the
manner, types and selection of services and merchandise
to be provided for the above named person needing
services, and to designate the place, form and final
disposition (including cremation) of the human remains of
the one named in need of services.

In witness whereof, I have voluntarily signed this Waiver,
the ___day of the month of _____

In the year of _____

_____ Name

_____ Address

_____ Relationship

_____ Witness

62

ACCOUNT LEDGER

DATE	DESCRIPTION	DEBIT	CREDIT	BALANCE

SAMPLE OBITUARY

Obiographical Sketch/Announcement for Media

Mr./Mrs./Ms./Uncle _____ at the age _____ succeeded many on _____, 20_____ at_____ hospital/home/institution.

Funeral services will be/were held on _____, 20_____ at _____ A.M. _____P.M.

Cause of death was_____

_____will be officiating.
Internment or Burial will/was held at
_____ Cemetery
located in (City) _____
(State)_____
Plot #_____

Memorial Services for _____

Will be or were held at
_____(church/funeral
chapel/park) located at _____
_____Direct
ions: _____

Mr./Mrs./Ms./Miss_____
leaves to celebrate his/her passing and heaven going:
_____wife/husband,
_____, _____ and _____

In the_____ family also are his/her
Brothers:_____ Sisters:_____
sisters-in-law _____ Brothers-in–law_____,
Great_____, Nieces_____
Nephews_____ and an enumerable host of
other relatives and friends. "The End!"

~Order of Service~

The Order Prelude

The Family Processional

The Opening Prayer

The Opening Scripture

The Selection

The Acknowledgement of Cards, Telegrams, and Condolences

The Reading of the Obituary-Church Clerk

The Remarks

The Selection

The Message of Comfort

The Parting View

The Benediction

THIS IS MY

"WILL"

How To Write Obiographical Sketches

(Your Own Obituaries)

The Resource Guide

Angelee Coleman Grider, author

Lizzie B. Davis, Funeral Director

ISBN 978-0-9801647-7-0

M.O.R.E. Publishers Corp.
St. Louis, MO 63138
MOREPublishersCO@AOL.com